# LET MY PEOPLE GO!

Tim Dowley

Illustrations by Gordon King

## Pharaoh the Great

Pharaoh, the ruler of the land of Egypt, was worried.
Why should he be worried?
He was very rich.
His land stretched for mile after mile along the banks of the great River Nile.
He was building many palaces, so that after he died people would say:
"Those were built by Pharaoh, the great ruler of Egypt."
But still he was worried.

## Hebrew slaves

Some of the people who lived in his land were called Hebrews.
Many Hebrews worked as Pharaoh's slaves, making bricks for his buildings.
Pharaoh was afraid that one day the Hebrews would stop working and fight against him.
So Pharaoh made plans to keep the Hebrews from becoming strong.
First he told his bosses:
"Don't let these Hebrew workers rest.
Punish them if they don't work hard enough.
You have whips – use them!"
Then he had another idea.
"Here is my new law," he said.
"Throw every Hebrew baby boy into the River Nile to die."

## The baby in the basket

Miriam and Aaron were very excited.
They had a new baby brother named Moses.
But Moses' mother was worried.
They were a Hebrew family, and she knew that Pharaoh had ordered all Hebrew baby boys to be thrown into the River Nile.
At first she hid the tiny baby in their little mud house.
But it was hard to keep the baby from crying and letting Pharaoh's soldiers know where he was hidden.

## Mother's plan

Then Moses' mother had an idea.
She called to Miriam:
"Go and fetch some reeds from the bank of the river."
Miriam brought back a big bundle of reeds, and Moses' mother wove them into a little basket.
When the basket was finished, she painted it with tar so that it would not let in water.
Then Miriam and her mother carried baby Moses and the basket to the edge of the river.
They laid Moses gently in the basket and covered him up.
Then they looked for a place among the reeds where they could safely leave the basket.
Miriam hid nearby to watch what happened next.

**The princess and the baby**

Miriam didn't have long to wait.
Very soon the princess of Egypt, Pharaoh's daughter, came down to bathe in the river.
Just as she reached the river's edge, the princess noticed the little basket in the reeds.
She sent one of her slave girls to get it.
When the princess opened the basket, baby Moses woke up and started to cry.
The princess picked him up and rocked him in her arms.
"Shhhh! Shhhh! There, there!"

**A brave sister**

The princess guessed it was a Hebrew baby, whose mother had put him there to keep him from being drowned in the river.
"We can't let him die," she said.
"So I'll take him back to my palace and bring him up as my own baby."
When she heard the princess say this, Miriam had an idea.
She came out of her hiding place.
"Your majesty," she said nervously.
"Would you like me to find a Hebrew woman who can nurse the baby for you?"
The princess said, "Yes, please do. And of course I will pay her well!"
So Miriam ran off and soon returned with the baby's mother.

**An Egyptian prince**

So Moses was safely brought up by his own mother.
When he grew up, the princess took him to live in the palace as an Egyptian prince.
But one day Moses saw an Egyptian boss beating a Hebrew slave.
This made him so angry that Moses knocked down the Egyptian and killed him.
Then Moses was afraid and ran away from Egypt to a far country.
No one there knew that he was an Egyptian prince.

**The bush that didn't burn up**

Moses found work as a shepherd.
One day, as he was leading his sheep, Moses noticed a bush on fire.
He looked again. No – he wasn't mistaken!
Although the bush was burning, it didn't burn up!
Moses went closer.
Then he a voice saying, "Moses! Moses!"
Moses said: "Here I am."
"Take off your sandals," said the voice, "because you are standing on holy ground.
I am God."
Moses was very frightened and covered his face.
But God gave him a special message:
"Moses, go to Pharaoh.
Tell him to let My people go!"

**Let My people go!**

When Moses heard God's message, he was terrified.
"How can I stand in front of Pharaoh and say, 'Let my people go!'?" he asked.
But God promised to help him.
"Your brother Aaron can go with you," God told him.
So Moses returned to Egypt.
He called together his people, the Hebrews, and told them that God was going to lead them out of Egypt into a land of their own.

**Pharaoh is angry**

Then Moses and Aaron went boldly to Pharaoh.
"Listen, Pharaoh," they said.
"The God of the Hebrews says, 'Let my people go!'"
But Pharaoh would not let them go.
"Who is this God?
Why should I obey him?
Why should I let my Hebrew slaves go?"
Pharaoh became very angry.
"Moses and Aaron," he shouted.
"Get back to your jobs!"
Then Pharaoh yelled at his slave bosses:
"From now on the Hebrews must not only make bricks; they must also gather up the straw to help make the bricks.
It seems they don't have enough work to do."

**Pharaoh changes his mind**

Pharaoh wouldn't let the Hebrews go, no matter how many times Moses came and asked.
So God brought ten troubles to the land of Egypt.
Each time one of these troubles happened, Pharaoh called Moses to him.
"All right, Moses," he would say.
"I know your God is making these things happen. Take your people and go."
But as soon as the trouble stopped, Pharaoh changed his mind.
He didn't want to lose all his best slaves.

**Ten troubles**

So ten troubles came to Egypt.
First, the water turned as red as blood and no one could drink it.
Second, thousands of frogs ran over the land.
Third, the land was filled with millions of gnats.
Fourth, clouds of flies flew everywhere.
Fifth, the Egyptians' animals became sick and died.
Sixth, people's bodies were covered with horrible boils.
Seventh, a terrible storm came, with hailstones so big they tore the leaves off trees.
Eighth, there came huge swarms of locusts – insects like grasshoppers that ate all the gardens in the land.
Ninth, Egypt was in darkness for three days.

**"Get out of my sight!"**

At last Pharaoh called Moses to him again.
"You can go; but you must not take your cattle, sheep, or goats with you."
"But God has told us to take them too," said Moses.
Pharaoh flew into a rage.
"Get out of my sight!
Don't ever appear before me again!
The day you see me you will die!"
Moses was quiet.
"Just as you say," he said. "I will never appear before you again."

**The tenth trouble**

Then came the tenth, and worst, trouble.
During the night the oldest boy in every Egyptian family died.
But no Hebrew children died that night.
The Hebrews had put lamb's blood over their doors, and God kept them safe.
In the Hebrews' homes, everyone was busy getting ready to leave Egypt.
They were in such a hurry that they baked flat bread; there was no time to let it rise!
They ate their last meal standing up, dressed for the journey.
In the darkness, the Hebrews left Egypt.
They were beginning the long journey that would take them to the land that God had promised to give them, the land of Canaan.

**Free at last!**

The Hebrews left Egypt joyfully.
At last they were free of Pharaoh and his cruel ways!
They took the road through the desert that led towards the Red Sea.
But they hadn't got far before Pharaoh changed his mind again.
*What am I thinking of, letting my best slaves escape?* he asked himself.
So he ordered his fastest chariots to chase the Hebrews.
They rode and rode without stopping.
At last they saw the Hebrews ahead of them.

**Across the Red Sea**
The Hebrews were terrified.
"Why have you brought us into the desert to die?" they asked Moses.
"We were better off as slaves in Egypt."
But Moses said: "Don't be afraid!
God will save us!"
And God held back the water of the Red Sea.
So Moses led the Hebrews across the dry bottom of the sea.
But when Pharaoh's chariots tried to follow them, they stuck fast.
And when the sea flowed back, Pharaoh's army drowned.

## A high mountain

When the Hebrews saw what had happened to the Egyptian army, they thanked God for saving them. Moses sang to the Lord in his joy.
But after that the Hebrews had months of hard marching through the desert.
After many, many miles they arrived at last at the foot of a tall mountain named Mount Sinai.
Moses climbed to the very top of Mount Sinai, which was hidden in clouds.
The people heard great rumbles of thunder and were very frightened.

## God's laws

When Moses reached the top, God spoke to him. He gave him ten special laws for the people, and Moses wrote them down.
God told the Hebrews they should not worship any other gods, or make idols and pray to them.
He told them they should keep one day in the week special for God.
He told them that they should respect their mothers and fathers.
And God told them not to cheat or treat other people badly.
Then Moses came down the mountain and read to his people the laws that God had given him.
When they heard them, the people said:
"We will obey God's laws and do as He tells us!"
So God led his people out of slavery in Egypt and towards the land he had promised them.

# For parents and teachers

**You can find this story in your Bible.**

Pharaoh the Great: Exodus 1:1-22
The baby in the basket: Exodus 2:1-10
An Egyptian prince: Exodus 2:11-15
The bush that didn't burn up: Exodus 3:1-22
Let My people go!: Exodus 4:1-17
Pharaoh is angry: Exodus 4:18-5:21
Pharaoh changes his mind: Exodus 7:14-10:29
Get out of my sight!: Exodus 11:1-12:39
Free at last!: Exodus 13:17-22
Across the Red Sea: Exodus 14:1-31
A high mountain: Exodus 19
God's laws: Exodus 20